BAND NERDS
Poetry From The 13th Chair Trombone Player

By DJ Corchin

"DJ must have been a fly on the wall of my band room for the last thirty years! I read, smiled and reflected on people who have all been a part of my band (and my life) over the years. Every once in a while, I found that I was looking in a mirror - and that made me smile, too. As you read these poems, you'll see the face and remember the name of each of these people... You'll remember the great times shared with all of the characters...heck, you may even remember the special smell of a well used band room...then you'll smile, too."

Greg Bimm
Director of Bands; Marion Catholic High School, Chicago Heights, IL

"I'm a band nerd. I admit it. My entire life has been spent playing in, conducting and teaching bands. I am in this book along with my friends, teachers and students. And you know what? DJ is right... they are special people and I like them all. It was a lot of fun to have my life reflected in this book."

Donald DeRoche
Director of Bands; DePaul Univeristy, Chicago, IL

"Coming from a professional 19th chair band geek who is still searching for her "ultimate mouthpiece," I can't think of a better way to cherish the unique inner world of life in the band! These poems prove that participation in school music goes beyond fulfilling an arts credit...it creates a sense of pride, belonging, and humor both on stage and off. Kudos to DJ for creating a hilarious and original work for anyone who has spent even just one day in band class!"

Amy McCabe
Trumpeter/Cornetist;
"The President's Own" United States Marine Band.

"'Band Nerds' is a look inside what must be the band room in every school - and a look back at my own inner band nerd. Even years removed, DJ's spot on humor brings a sheepish smile to my face as I remember those days and all the 'characters' that have been part of MY music history."

Scott McCormick
President and CEO of Music for All, Inc.
and the Bands of America and Orchestra America divisions

"DJ Corchin's book provides a rare, in-depth insight into our nation's band sub-culture, a medium that continues to provide emotional sanctuary for so many of our best and brightest young people. His poetry opens a window for us former band members to reflect fondly upon our school years, while it also garners an opportunity for the rest of the world to understand the powerful force which drives so many of us to success in life."

Dave Morrison
Illinois Teacher of the Year 2003 and Director of Bands (retired);
Prospect High School, Mt Prospect, IL

"What a KICK! You'll find yourself laughing and sometimes crying at the wonderful words DJ Corchin has articulately and artfully put on paper in this collection of poems. Using the power of poetry anyone who is in band, was in band, knows someone in band, or knew someone in band will enjoy this book. Whether humorous or harsh, poignant or pathetic, inspiring or irritating - either way DJ hopes you will choose to 'laugh it off.' Helping the reader to rise above the stereotyping that unfortunately sometimes shapes our perceptions and personalities, this book taps into the healthy therapeutic nature of humor to laugh with - and sometimes at - the wonderfully strange world of Band Nerds."

Fran Kick
Educational consultant,
speaker and author who inspires kids to KICK IT IN®

"Being a member of a band family made the high school years bearable! These poems bring back so many memories as they perfectly describe my time in the flute section. (Thank GOD I switched to bassoon!) This would have been THE book to read when skipping English class... hanging out in the band room of course! A must read for band students both young and old."

Camilla M. Stasa
Director of Participant Relations, Music for All (Bands of America)

"This fun, humorous, interesting, journey through life via membership in the band is a delightful read. These poems joggled my memory and took me back to many wonderful friends, places and sounds. Change the names and this is my life. At times we've all stood out, couldn't get it, and/or the entire world was conspiring against us. It's called growing up and these poems capture the entire exciting roller coaster ride, providing you were fortunate enough to find the band room during your childhood. Enjoy, smile, laugh and be thankful, you were in the band!"

Brian Logan
Director of Bands; Wheeling High School, Wheeling, IL

BAND NERDS
Poetry From The 13th Chair Trombone Player

By DJ Corchin

The phazelFOZ Company, LLC

Published by The phazelFOZ Company, LLC.
Chicago, Illinois
www.phazelfoz.com

Illustrations, book, and jacket design by Dan Dougherty
Edited by Mike Hurley

Library of Congress Number 2009901301

ISBN 978-0-9819645-0-8 (Paperback)

Dedicated to

Dr. Wesley Vos
L.J. Hancock
&
Jonathan "Lance" Harmeling

Stereotypes

We all know stereotypes can have a terrible effect. They're harmful to a person's ego, self-worth, and self-esteem. There's nothing more frustrating than being categorized before someone even takes the time to talk with you. Whether it involves race, gender, age, religion, sexuality, or something as small as what activities you're in, stereotypes are unfortunately here to stay. There's not going to be a huge revolution of the human mind that says, "You know what? I don't need to categorize things within 3 seconds of seeing them." So the only weapon we have against stereotypes, in this non-doctor's, non-psychologist's, non-philanthropist's, non-professor's, non-philosopher's opinion, is *choice*. We can choose to let them shape us, or we can choose to write a silly poem book about them and laugh it off. You choose.

13th Chair

I was 13th chair in my elementary band.
I was as discouraged as I could be.
The teacher told me it was alphabetized,
But my name starts with C.

And as time went on, I never moved.
Last chair is where I'd sit.
But 7 years later I'm finally first
'Cause everyone else had quit.

Distress Call

Hello 911? Please help me
I don't know what to do!
My band is spinning out of control,
The room's become a zoo.
There's so much going on right now
I'm not sure where to start.
Jenny lit her reeds on fire,
The tuba lit his fart.
The trombones are in the corner
Playing truth or dare.
Which I guess explains
Why John McBain
Is in his underwear.
There's French Horns in the rafters.
Piccolos breaking stands.
Saxes kissing one another,
And baritones eating crayons.

The percussion are hosting a seance,
I'm scared for my life.
Oh God they have a dead goat over there
And a picture of my wife!
The trumpets are in the practice room,
But not to practice early.
They grabbed a freshman by the toes
And proceeded with a swirly.
I've lost control. I'm not in charge.
Come quick it can't be far.
Please they're banging down my office door
With the muffler of my car!

Enough

I didn't really believe it,
'Til I looked in and seen it,
But nevertheless it's true.
Tom's tuba could talk,
It got up and walked,
And said, "the heck with you I'm through."

Ultimate Mouthpiece

Now and forever
My mistakes shall cease,
'Cause I bought myself
An ultimate mouthpiece.
Never again will I miss a note,
Will you hear a gerplat,
A patoot, or a splote.
I place it in my horn,
It's magic you'll see,
'Cause my fingers move
Faster than faster can be.
...did I mention I can now hit a double quadruple G!
Even though I'm only twelve
A hundred grand at least,
Is what I should be paid for me
To play my ultimate mouthpiece.

Euphonium

Nothing rhymes with euphonium.
Except the word plutonium.
So I'll just use euphonium
And finally write this poem.

Revenge

It's ok to gawk and laugh out loud
Making fun of me a bit.

I'll just place my spit valve on your head
Count to three and let'er rip!

New Private Teacher

Wow thank you Mrs. Nevenshire.
You were sent from heaven.
Jimmy plays three times a day
Since you teach all his lessons.

I Have An Itch

I have an itch.
I have an itch.
I can not scratch
Or move an inch.
I'm at attention.
I can not twitch.
Oh what to do.
I have an itch.

Closed Eyes

I'd like to tell you about a friend
I met last year this time.
He was a pretty special kid
You see my friend is blind.

That didn't stop him from playing his horn
He just listened once and knew it.
He'd close his eyes and finger along
I'm not sure how he'd do it.

I asked him why he closed his eyes
His answer quite profound.
He said, "People tend to stare at them,
Not focus on my sound."

I thought, how true the world we have
We look before we listen.
Maybe if we closed our eyes
The world would pay attention.

From Me To You

Musical. Instrument. Digital. Interface.
Think it up. Plug it in. Send it off to cyberspace.
Post it up. Send it out. Surf around. Find the link.
Grab the tune. Plug it in. Start it up and data sync.

I Seem To Have A Problem 1

I seem to have a problem.
I'm not sure where to start.
Every time I play my oboe
I also play a fart.

The Great Kiss Off of '96

The great kiss off contest of '96
Was the best that's ever been.
Pride was at stake for the hearts of the band
To quit was a mortal sin.

Faces were red, cheeks were blown,
Eyes popped out of their sockets.
But nothing compared to Jared DuCaine
And the trick he pulled out of his pocket.

He stepped to the crowd all smiley and proud
And took out his special mouthpiece.
Unbelievably small it measured around
The size of a straw at least.

Jared put it to his face, buckled down hard,
Took a big breath and blew.
A screeching E flat was the note that he picked
And boy it came barreling through.

At first he was normal, even cool and calm,
But then he began to change.
His eyes started to water, his knees shook,
You could tell that he was in pain.

But that didn't stop Big Jared - no way
As the sweat dripped down from his nose.
Bulges began to pop from his head
And air shot out of his toes.

He started leaking fluids
From every place and more-so.
His left eye shot out, he blew a vein,
A rib popped out of his torso.

But Jared kept playing even louder
Until he finally just gave out.
He ripped the sucker off his face
And took off half his mouth.

The crowd erupted and rose to their feet,
As the hero picked up his lips.
His feat would be called an historic event.
The Great Kiss Off Of '96.

Guard Captain

This girl said she was guard captain.
I had reason not to believe her.
She claimed to be able to throw a twelve
So I said I'd like to see her.
With a bend of the knee and a twist of the wrist,
The saber cut through the air.
She ran in fear
As it sliced her ear
A sight I could not bear.

I Got Your Pass Right Here!

I'm sorry I'm late to math class,
But it really wasn't my fault.
Our director made us march ahead
And refused to give a halt.
We must have gone six miles,
Through mud and sleet and snow.
We jumped a fence and swam a creek,
Climbed mountains high and low.
He made us march past Jimmy's house.
You know, the one with the rabid dog?
It chased us for at least eight blocks.
We lost it in the fog.
By the time we made it back to school,
There were broken bones and shattered glass.
The nurse amputated my left toe,
So do you really need a pass?

Saxes In Concert Band

Play Softer! Play Softer!
That's all they ever say.
They tell me to play piano,
But it's written forte.

And when I raise my hand
To tell them what's there,
They say, "you're saxes in concert band,
I really don't care."

The Triangle Player From Del Torre

I am the triangle player from Del Torre.
Everybody knows my story.
With a ting and a ping
I make women sing,
'Cause I am the triangle player from Del Torre.

16

Operation

Mom, oh Mom, can I please get
That special operation?
The one that allows you to play the trombone
As a full time occupation.

What do you mean you don't understand?
Where do you think the slide goes?
It goes down your throat
and out your rear
My brother told me so.

Drummer

Flam tap, Flam tap, Flam tap, Splot!
Flam Accent, Flam Accent, Shot!
I can drum in perfect beat.
Paradittle, paradittle, kiss my feet.

Rough, Rough, Rough, Flog
Now you're sounding like a dog.
Herta, Herta, Herta, smack.
I'll put a drum stick in your crack.

Scale Test

Why do we have to learn the hard ones?
We never see more than 4 flats.
That's like telling us we're gonna use
All the lessons learned in math.

And we only ever see a sharp
If we're orchestra volunteers.
Why should we be penalized
For helping out our peers?

The key of B is meaningless,
To me it's just plain wrong.
How about I stick with C
And we can move along.

Drum MAJOR Crush

I love it when she yells at me.
I lose it when she looks at me.
She tells me what to do you see
And puts me in my spot.

Turn right, flank left, toes off the ground.
I love she bosses me around.
The stricter that she gets I've found
The more I think she's hot.

My Uniform

I got it! I got it!
I got it today!
My uniform is here.
Hoorah! Hooray!

So what it's too big.
So what it's too small.
So what that it smells
And don't fit at all.

It's mine, I'm happy.
It's mine I say.
My uniform is here.
Hoorah! Hooray!

Secret Weapon

An army recruiter came by yesterday
I'm really not sure why.
He watched us spin our rifles 'round
Then pointed to the sky.

He wanted us to join his ranks.
Airborne unit he said.
I had to tell him the guns weren't real
And this was all pretend.

But he didn't care 'bout the guns in the air
So I started to hold my breath.
He said, "We'll drop you in, forget your spins,
Just talk them all to death."

True Friends

I'm not sure why we did it.
But we did it nonetheless.
We locked our friend up in the john,
Shut the lights and left.

He happened to play tuba,
So it was clear that he was missing.
We continued to play our warm-up scales
While he was reminiscing.

The teacher asked us where he was.
We shook our heads about.
We hadn't decided either way,
If we would let him out.

Skip

I met a tuba player named Skip.
I tried to giv'm a tip.
No matter how hard he tried,
He sat there and sighed,
'Cause he only had one lip.

Inspiration

First of all, congrats to you
For making it all this way.
We've come so far if you recall
And remember our first day.

And now we're here at concert time.
So exciting from the start.
Just remember all you've learned
And make the music from your heart.

I know you expect a story or two
To inspire you for luck.
I'm not quite sure what's left to say,
But whatever you do, don't suck.

I Seem To Have A Problem 2

I seem to have a problem
I'm not sure why it is.
Once I put my uniform on
I have to take a whiz.

First Chair

I am the first chair.
A very important role.
Everyone looks up to me.
At least that's what I'm told.

I have special duties
Passing music to the rest.
I am the first chair I say
Of all the 3rd part clarinets.

Challenge

I challenge you, you stupid fool
Tomorrow right at noon.
You'll lose your chair and I'll sit there
Before I'm through with you.

        I challenge YOU, you petty turd.
        Yes that's right, I said it.
        You suck, by luck you got real close
        And now you're gonna get it.

Oh please you tool, I'll walk right in
And put you right to tears.
Mentally you'll be a wreck.
Need therapy for years.

        You challenge me? Are you insane?
        I can't imagine why.
        I'll smack your sister in her face
        And make your mother cry!

28

The Opener

I think you should play percussion.
I'm not sure flute is for you.
Not trumpet, horn, or saxophone.
None of these will do.

How can I put this nicely?
How can I say this right?
Um, you could open a can of soup
With your massive overbite.

Juggernaut

Westmoore High School won again
But it's really no surprise.
They've never ever ever lost.
In this I tell no lies.

Their director served the army.
Their guard captain on Broadway.
Between the two, they tend to spend
More cash than Uruguay.

Their drums are made of solid gold.
Flags tailored by Versace.
Their meals prepared and catered by
The famous chef Lagasse.

They rent the entire Astrodome
For a Wednesday night rehearsal.
Their performances filmed and marketed by
The staff at Universal.

There's no secret why they won.
No one stood a chance.
They could afford a jet to fly
The judges all to France.

Magic Oboe

Yesterday I sat down and played
What I thought was a normal B flat.
But when I made a sound
I looked to the ground.
Scott Miller morphed into a rat!

I thought, "this is cool, the power I have,"
And proceeded to have some fun.
I played a low G
And that jerk Tom McGee
Was suddenly dressed as a nun.

I couldn't resist and had to persist
To give all the tubas green hair.
The saxes were dead
The flutes had no legs
And suddenly I was first chair!

I play a magic oboe.
Don't laugh, you know what I'll do?
I'll tap on the keys
And blow on the reeds
So your mouthpiece tastes like poo!

I Suck

Oh man not again, I cracked a note
And my valve? Yep, it stuck.
I can't tongue for spit
I must admit.
Jeez, I really suck.

Secret Room

Deep behind the band room
There's a room we like to store
Our instruments and costume racks
But that's not what it's for.

Only students enter in.
Teachers do not dare.
We call it the secret make out room
Guess what we do there?

Stuck

My saber's stuck in a star up high
It's lost somewhere up in the sky.
If you see it sticking out,
Please tell me of it's whereabouts.

Jazzer

I don't play that kind
Of music I find
It's just not appealing to me.

I don't march in line
Play 8th notes in time
Jazz is my gig, you see.

Mr. Smith

Beware of Mr. Smith
Director of the band.
He can make you poop your pants,
With a single stroke of his hand.
He's fat, he's bald, he has fake teeth,
At least that I can tell.
The yellow sweat stains under his arms
Have finally begun to smell.
Once in a while he'll give you a smile
But anyone will tell ya,
You can't trust him because that grin
Means he's gonna fail ya.

Band Dads

What do you need, what can I move?
Is there something I can getch'ya?
No one moves faster than me and my crew,
If you do it's 'cause we letch'ya.
We've hauled percussion through sleet and snow,
Through hail and acid rain.
There's no job too heavy or task too hard
For we do not feel pain.
Dedication runs through our veins
For our children's musical lives.
The more time we spend catering to them,
The less we do with our wives!

F and B Flat

Will everyone please play
An F and B flat?
That's all that I want.
An F and B flat.
You don't need to laugh
At something like that.
Will someone please play
AN F'n B FLAT!?

Awkwardly Band

I recently joined the awkwardly band,
That's led by an equally awkwardly man.
It has a unique and awkwardly sound.
It's where the weird people are awkwardly found.

One boy plays an awkward recorder
And seems to have an awkward disorder.
No wonder he's in the awkwardly band.
He seems to play with three awkwardly hands.

And there's the girl who's awkwardly shy.
We think it's because of her awkwardly eyes.
It's not that they're black or awkwardly red.
But they're on the wrong side of her awkwardly head.

It's awkwardly awkward to play in this place,
With it's awkwardly style and awkwardly taste.
Awkwardly led by that awkwardly man,
I recently joined the awkwardly band.

On Fire

"Jimmy why are you moving?
The whole band's at a halt."

        "I'm sorry sir, but I have to say,
          It's really not my fault."

"Oh no, who else is running around
As if they were on fire?"

        "That's the point I'm trying to make,
          The situation's kind of dire."

I Seem To Have A Problem 3

I seem to have a problem.
I'm not sure what to git.
If I play the clarinet
I suck up my own spit?!

The Letter

Dear Mom,
    I'm writing to you today because
    I have a tiff with how you raised me.
    I don't understand, I do all I can
    And no one seems to praise me.
    I play high notes, the kind that screech,
    My scales at two-twenty-two.
    I play my trumpet perfectly
    So the problem must be with you.
    Please don't be mad or even sad,
    I'm being honest like you taught me.
    Just admit how bad you screwed up
    And I'll put this all behind me.

(The Reply)

Dear Son,
    You're dumb, you stupid fool,
    Idiotic I'd say at best.
    Don't blame me because they see
    You're more obnoxious than the rest.
    You wouldn't listen all those years.
    Just blew louder in my face.
    I'm glad that all the pretty girls
    Put your sorry butt in place.
    And as long as we're being honest
    There's something that should be said.
    Don't talk to me again like that.
    I know you wet your bed.

Hmm...

She's looking at me
'Cross the band once again.
Is she smiling or squeezing out
That note at measure 10?

French Horns are so confusing.
Are they happy or are they mad?
They always seem to make a face
Both joyful and somewhat sad.

If she could just tell me
What she's thinking either way.
I'll know to either run like hell,
Or ask her out today.

47

Hope

I wanna tell you something.
I'm not sure if I should.
Something I'm not proud of.
Something that's not good.

I think I've fallen really hard
For someone not in band.
I know I'm not supposed to but,
She's gorgeous, tall, and tan.

I see her after school sometimes
Hanging with her guy.
I hope one day I'll live to say
I actually said hi.

I Seem To Have A Problem 4

I seem to have a problem.
I'm not sure who to tell.
Every time I play the trumpet
My ego hurts like hell.

Busting Out

I didn't want to say it
But your uniform's too small.
Your bosom's really busting out
And we can see it all.

49

A Truly Weird Audition

I want center snare
Not because of my flare
Or due to my natural wit.

I truly believe
That I can achieve
Perfection while down in the splits.

Toes Up

I never thought I'd see the day
Someone's toes too high.
But Alex's feet were straight up and down,
I couldn't believe my eyes.

The Pit Crew From Calmanti

Our pit crew from Calmanti
Is known throughout the land,
We're able to move in 10 seconds flat
And build apartments for the band.
We have only the best parents
Recruited for this routine,
With physical training and strategy plans
We're a well oiled machine.

Mr. Jones the nuclear physicist.
He builds our jet powered carts.
Mr. Sindle runs the mafia,
So he steals all our parts.
Mr. Briar works at NASA,
For satellite communications.
Mrs. Niles is a supreme court judge
And handles accusations.

Mr. Grell works at the Pentagon
To get our fake I.D.s.
Mrs. Landy's in the CIA
For operations over-seas.
Mikey Keller's cousin
Flies Stealths and F-16s.
Mr. Trent is in command
Of a Navy Submarine.

The Pit Crew from Calmanti
Is a legend near and far.
Our tales are often midnight dreams,
And stories told at bars.

There's no job we can not handle.
No country we can not run.
But if all you need is percussion moved
Consider it already done.

Journey

We went to contest the other day
And the judges said we stunk.
But I would have to disagree
That what we did was junk.

We spent 3 months just practicing
For the pieces we would play.
We felt ourselves improve a bit
Each and every day.

When we started out this year
No one played a scale.
Now we play all twelve of them
Before the Bach Chorales.

It doesn't matter what they say
With their ridicule and scorn.
The judges don't mean squat to us
'Cause we finally play our horns.

Women.

I had to break it off with Jill.
It really wouldn't work.
It's not my fault I made top band.
But apparently <u>I'm</u> the jerk.

She said if I really loved her
I wouldn't have done so good.
We'd both be in the low band,
Like the way a couple should.

Well, I told her she was crazy.
Farewell, goodbye, so long.
It's not my fault she sucked at flute,
But apparently <u>I</u> was wrong.

Hot Cross Buns

Hot...Cross...Buns.
Hot...Cross...Buns.
I can not believe I'm doing
This...is...dumb.

I Seem To Have A Problem 5

I seem to have a problem.
I'm not sure what to do.
I want to play percussion
But have no attitude.

Old Fashioned

No girl will be in my snare line.
Not while I'm alive.
That doesn't seem to work for me.
With her I can not thrive.
She'll screw up all the chemistry.
It's always been us dudes.
Plus, the harness couldn't possibly fit
Over her gigantic boo...um...hair.
It's not that I'm against all girls
Or hate women you see.
It's that most of them in our band
Well, they just play better than me!

John McDoogal

There's John McDoogal
Who plays on his flugel,
The sweet sweet sounds of the blues.

He'll play there all night
For the women in sight.
There's no way he could possibly lose.

But the jokes played on him
As the women all grin
And wink at John in surprise.

The ladies all laughed
As he let out a gasp
And noticed his wide open fly.

Carpenters

Double reeds walk the line.
This we've always known.
They don't buy their reeds, the heck with that,
They go and make their own.

They chisel away for hours on end,
Skilled with chunks of wood.
I'd hire them to build my house.
I really think they could.

Microphone

Mr. Harris swallowed his microphone
And he just can't get it free.
So we hear him almost all the time.
Like when he has to pee.

We've heard him with the principal.
We've heard him passing gas.
We've heard him singing stupid songs
And kissing Mrs. Nash!

2nd Chair Princess

Now you listen here
Mr. Band Director man.
I should be first chair
Not that horse with a tan.
Are you nuts? Are you blind?
Are you feeling ok?
There's no way she beat me.
You're wrong all the way.
She's stupid, she's ugly,
She's the world's biggest nerd.
She's the joke of the town.
Have you not heard?
I'm so much better.
You can't even compare.
Her fashion is terrible
Not to mention her hair.
So I can't play my scales
And can't match a tone.
It won't mean a thing
When I get my mom on the phone.

Pride

I am the trumpet player.
I can play high.
I am the trumpet player,
With a gleam in my eye.
I can play loud.
I can play tough.
I love to play fast.
I can't get enough.
There's no part too hard,
Too tricky, too sly.
No one plays better than me.
I'd rather die.
I am the trumpet player.
I am the best.
Don't step to me 'cause
I'll turn your sorry butt inside out,
Kick you in your face and make sure you cry
so long your mamma is embarrassed to call you her child.

Joe

Joe talks too much about our band.
We think that he's obsessed.
Joe doesn't really date that much.
I'm sure you could've guessed.

Salute

Excuse me nurse do you have some ice?
I'm sorry I'm starting to cry.
It seems that when I saluted the crowd,
I hit myself right in the eye.

Saxamaphone

Saxamaphone, Saxamaphone,
I play the saxamaphone.
It sounds really neat
'Cause I have no teeth
When I play my saxamaphone.

School Horn

I brought home my new school horn today.
I opened it up almost right away.
My gosh that funk!
It stinks like skunk!
I brought back my new school horn today.

The Ghost of That's Freshman Pete

There's a legend that goes back about 80 years.
Before there's computers and mp3 gear.
A freshman joined band and on his first week,
He became known as That's Freshman Pete.

Horns would go up, his would go down.
They would go left, and he'd turn around.
The whole band would march
And come to a turn,
But Pete would keep going
Not even concerned.
He marched to his own
Awkwardly beat.
But they would just shrug
'Cause That's Freshman Pete.

Until one day, they came to a curve.
Pete kept on going, it was really absurd.
Normally he would stop and return,
But this time was different, real cause for concern.

Sooner than later he marched from their sight.
He didn't come back all day or all night.
In fact he didn't come back ever again,
And nobody knew what happened to him.

It's been said that since that day,
He still haunts this school today.
His ghost still marches in the streets,
Don't be scared, That's Freshman Pete.

Mistake

Did you hear that?
He cracked the G sharp.
I mean he's a pro
and <u>still</u> missed his part.

I don't care if he's nice,
I don't care if he's good.
I paid forty bucks,
So he'll play like he should.

No I won't settle down,
This isn't a joke.
He's getting paid
And I'm really broke!

True Player

All the ladies want to date me.
It's because I play trombone.
Ever since I switched from sax
They just won't leave me alone.

Torture

I love to mess with Greg Tulaine
Who lives with perfect pitch.
I'll dip my lips a quarter tone
Just to watch him twitch.

I know it bugs him really bad,
So of course I push it more.
Once I hit a half a step he
Starts convulsing on the floor.

Yes it seems a little cruel,
But it's something he deserves.
He always says I'm out of tune,
Can you believe his nerve?

Useless Talent

Have you seen the dancing euphonium player
Who plays for Blayton Prep?
They say he's able to do 4 turns
And not fall out of step.

He leaps, he twirls, he pops and locks
With toes that touch the clouds.
He'll play a heart felt melody
And "robot" for the crowds.

It's pretty darn amazing
What this guy can do.
But there's no jobs for dancing euphonium players
I know of none, do you?

Bad Day

My day is going really bad
I'm not sure why that is.
I failed my test with a 42
And fought with my friend Liz.

I tripped while walking to P.E.
And everyone just laughed.
I couldn't remember my locker's code
So I kicked it 'till it cracked.

My boyfriend dumped me during lunch
He did it in a note.
We had to do a fire drill
And someone stole my coat.

I walked into the bathroom,
But the stalls there had no doors.
It didn't take me long to see
The urinals weren't decor.

I find it's really hard to smile
I'm not sure how I can.
But things are looking better now
'Cause I'm on my way to hand.

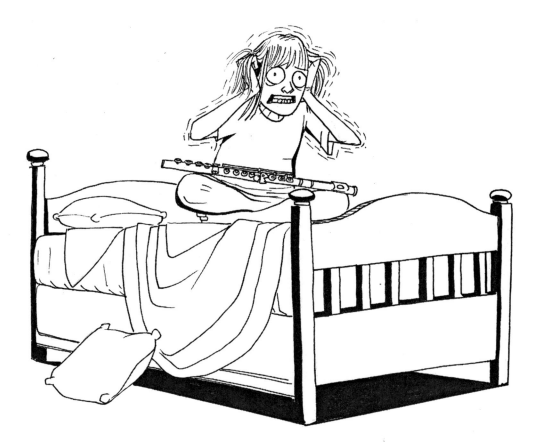

Audition

It was once said
That lying in bed
A little girl went nuts.
'Cause she stayed up all night
And trembled in fright
Her audition turned out a bust.

How A Trumpet Plays A Duet

Let's play a duet.
Let's play it today.
I'll play the high part
And you go away.

Disturbing

I think of band all the time,
I think of it in the shower.
I think of it while I'm rehearsing a play
Or outside picking flowers.

I think of band while playing catch
And almost all I do.
But what's really weird is I think of band
While making out with you!

Natural High

I love the sound of low notes
On my flute that I just bought.
They sound so rich and lovely.
Just like I was taught.

I've become renowned for them.
The low note player in town.
I would play them all the time,
But I get dizzy, then fall down.

Medieval Marching

This year's show was a medieval theme
And quite a sight to bear.
Every detail true in fact
And no expense was spared.

We played the extra long trumpets.
Like ones way back in the day.
They didn't have a single valve
One key is all we played.

Somehow we got 3 horses.
Which was very cool at first.
But then we stepped in something brown.
We're sure it wasn't dirt.

The costumes were made of sheep skin.
The jousting was done for real.
The swords landed just one cut.
It was really no big deal.

Then the staff went way too far.
It was a little bit upsetting.
They said for extra G.E. points
We should stage a real beheading!

Juggle

I like to juggle mouthpieces.
I can juggle up to four.
One hit me in the head today.
I don't juggle anymore.

Potential

Yesterday some would say
I received the kiss of death.
Mr. Logan gave the "potential speech"
To me and Jessica Beth.

He said I had "potential."
Whatever the heck that means.
All's I know he didn't pick me
To drive our marching machine.

But he wouldn't let me quit.
I'm not sure how he did it.
He somehow made me change my mind
I simply must admit it.

He told me that I need the band
As much as it needs me.
He was right I must confess
My potential he did see.

Mellophone, Mellophone

Mellophone, Mellophone,
Why do you smellophone?
You can't play in tuneophone.
Too gross to touch.

Mellophone, Mellophone,
What is your dealophone?
Valves are all stuckophone.
I hate you so much.

Balance and Blend

Balance and Blend,
Balance and Blend,
That is the key
To music my friend.

Poor April

What the heck is that?
A duck or crying goose?
No, it must be April Smith,
I guess her reed is loose.

83

Love-Hate Relationship

What are they doing
Those people back there?
I don't understand them,
They're crazy I swear.
They're loud, they smell,
There's no trace of tact.
They just wiped a booger
All over my back.
They sit there during rehearsal
And count their dumb rests.
The buttheads won't take
Their eyes off my chest.
They drool, they sweat.
A bath? What's that?
They bang on their drums
And poisoned my cat.

They lose all their sticks
Spill pop on the floor.
My gosh, what is that?
A dead rat on the door?
They give out free wedgies
And spit just for laughs.
Tommy the snare drum
Has really bad gas.
They rant and they rave
Hurt people for money.
Most of them think
Diarhhea is funny.
They give me the willies
I just want to puke.
Actually, now that I think about it...
them they are kinda cute.

Feet

I have unbelievably large feet
So it's easy to march to the beat.
It takes me less time,
To reach my yard line,
But it's hard to be discreet.

Clarinet Jack

Clarinet Jack is what he likes to be called,
With a reed in his mouth when walking the halls.
It's so he can feel that he's always prepared
When Clarinet Jack is needed.

He walks with a cool, confident strut.
And jeans wrap around his cool, confident butt.
He won't let you down no matter the cost
Our expectations are always exceeded.

Confidence

I'm sick and tired of getting punched
Because you don't understand.
You jocks just walk all over me
Because I play in band.
But no longer will you point and gawk,
I've had it up to here.
I don't think you heard me son,
Or else you'd run in fear.
I'm tough, I'm strong, been working out,
I've clearly found my niche.
I'd go so far as to say
I think your mom's a witch.
No no, stay there, no need to swear
Or charge at me like that.
I'll intimidate you with my built-up pecs
...or at least my brand new bat!

From Bad Audition To Worse

Mom, I know I didn't make the band.
At least with scores you see.
I heard the others play their parts.
They sounded better than me.

But mysteriously I made the cut.
I'm currently first chair.
You put on extra makeup.
Spent an hour on your hair.

I know you want the best for me
And I know I let you down.
Forgive me but I have to ask,
DID YOU HIT ON MR. BROWN?!

Advice

Um, you might want to get off the ground.
It's not where you want to sit.
I know you're not familiar with band,
But that's where we drain our spit.

Annoying

I think I'm finally gonna crack'm
If he doesn't stop his tap'n.
Jam my reed
Into his knee,
Kick him then I'll slap'm.

Hot Tub

I shared an awkward moment
With my high school band director.
The story's true I swear to God.
I'll take a lie detector.

I remember it quite clearly.
It was during freshman trip.
The band had gone to some place warm
And I played in the pit.

I woke up hearing talking
At 3:15 a.m.
I opened up my hotel door
And joined the gather'n.

It was me and him plus Tom McLil
And Joe I think was there.
We looked out at the hot tub pool
And we began to stare.

I have to say it shocked us all
What we saw in that tub.
The birds and bees were out that night
The moon shined high above.

He looked at us, we looked at him.
Not knowing what to say.
We bonded for the first time.
Those strangers made our day.

So we closed our doors, went back to bed
And never brought it up.
But we all remember "hot tub" night
As the night we all grew up.

Rookie Band Trip

Something's different about Mr. Sprant.
He just hasn't been the same.
He's been a little "off the beat,"
Since our trip to Spain.
Something about him is peculiar and odd.
Things are just not right.
His hands are shaking, his neck is aching
He claims he's losing his sight.
He blacks out on occasion,
Increased medication,
And sometimes tends to drool.
He used to have hair,
But now he is bare,
Oh how two weeks can be so cruel.

The New Drum Major

Get your toes up!
Get'm up high!
I wanna see the gum on your shoes
And your chin at the sky!
Get those shoulders back buddy,
And suck in that gut.
Put the cheeseburger down
And don't be a klutz.
What's wrong with you kid
That you can't do a flank?
Not heard of deodorant?
You smell kinda rank.
Your technique is all wrong
You're playing is poo,
You look like my dad's butt
Which has zits just like you.
Get yourself at attention.
I didn't say at ease.
Wait Mom, I'm not done yet,
Don't go, I'm just practicing. Come on, Please?

95

The Ringer

Our lead Alto's Grant Van Singer.
The famous, handsome, jazz soloist ringer.
His notes are so quick,
His licks are so sick,
You won't even notice his four extra fingers.

Too Cool

We read this tune in Jazz band.
It had an amazing groove.
It was so laid back, we couldn't play
So we sat and didn't move.

The whole rehearsal seemed to pass
But it didn't really matter.
The point is that we're being cool
And we'll be called a "jazzer."

I Seem To Have A Problem 6

I seem to have a problem.
I really have to say.
My slide got bent to 90 degrees
Which makes it hard to play.

Tough Love

I love my flute
I love it this much!
I hug it every day
And treat it as such.

I bring it to the store,
To the park, to the zoo.
Why it won't play,
I don't have a clue.

My First Parade

Oh my gosh I'm out of step.
My posture's bad as bad can get.
My toes aren't up, my knees are stiff,
I can not feel my upper lip.
I can't remember all my parts.
I have no clue of where to start.
I think my bibbers lost a clip,
My drawers are out and I might trip.

Lost

I'm no longer a freshman
But still have some questions
And still need some help on my parts.

And I'm not quite a junior
If you don't help me soon you're
Liable to see me depart.

Not sure where I fit in
This band that I sit in
Someone just tell me my place.

A sophomore this season I
Don't see the reason why
Seniors are still in my face.

Just Try It

Go ahead and try it.
Just try it for a week.
Grab a horn and join the band,
Release your inner geek.

Live the life that we live.
Practice night and day.
You just might find you're getting good,
And maybe want to stay.

Famous Last Words

It's not me, honestly.
It's the reed you see
Making me squawk and squeak.
I practiced really hard I swear.
Like 17 minutes last week.

Band Camp

I've heard all the jokes.
I've heard all the lines.
But it doesn't make me frown.

I go to band camp
Once a year,
'Cause man can we get down!

Best Friend

My tuba and me are best of friends,
But not because we talk.
We don't go to movies, braid our hair,
Or take a friendly walk.

It's been good to me ever since,
My mother went to buy it.
It plays in tune, it shines itself.
I even fit inside it.

So when I'm feeling really down,
And need a place to stay.
I crawl inside my tuba bell,
And hang out for the day.

Crazy Drill

This drill is completely crazy.
Dangerous to say the least.
It's got tubas rolling over snares,
And trumpets doing leaps.

The pit is marching on the field.
The guard up in the stands.
The saxes on the field goal posts.
The flutes ride in a van.

There seems to be a bassoon out there.
Ooo...that had to hurt.
Someone call a doctor quick
Or at least a certified nurse.

There's at least three pass thrus, which isn't bad,
Except they're every beat.
I can't read English quite as fast
As I have to move my feet.

I guess it's worth it in the end,
When the audience feels inspired.
But I'm still not sure we need to have
A burning ring of fire!

Choosing Time

The trumpet is too loud.
The flute is too high.
The violin's too screechy,
And the drums make me cry.

The tuba's too fat.
The oboe is sick.
I can't bear to hear
A licorice stick.

The piano's too plain.
The sax is too gold.
The bassoon is too weird looking
And too hard to hold.

The baritone's too boring
And reeks a foul stench.
The french horn is so stupid
I'M NOT EVEN FRENCH!

I wanna play an instrument.
I'm not sure which one.
There are so many to choose from
But most are just dumb.

The cello's too big
And I hate to sing.
Did I mention that music's
My favorite thing?

Podium

Mr. Block's podium
Is five and a half feet tall.
He says it's so we can see him well,
But I don't think that's all.

I think there's something up there.
Something we don't know.
We seem to hear strange noises
While he conducts us with his toes.

I Seem To Have A Problem 7

I seem to have a problem.
I'm not sure where to go.
I always play way out of tune.
My teacher told me so.

Skat

Do ba do dot
BaSquee ba do zot
Ba ratata boom, sha boom.

Veetle do dam,
Sha eetle rum sham
Ba Fatata shoom, ba oom.

Secret Envy

Being the low brass type
I just don't admit,
Thinking of woodwinds.
I'd have to quit.

But there's one thing
I wish I could have.
The fingerless gloves
Just...feel...so..."bad."

The New 4th Trumpet

"Sally, what is Jimmy doing here
 With that guilty little smear
  Which makes my bloodstream boil?"

"Well he got switched from third
 After they heard
  He likes to drink valve oil."

The Plea

I don't want to switch to bassoon,
I like playing the flute.
I won't play that ugly thing,
Not me, I'm way too cute.

I mean there's like a hundred pieces!
That's way too many parts.
I wouldn't know just what to do.
I'm really not that smart.

What the heck's a bocal?
Some green growth on your toe?
The buttons are too spread out,
And I refuse to play that low.

My parents smoke like crazy,
That wouldn't be so good.
'Cause the only instruments we have
Are all made from wood.

So please don't make me switch.
I'm really not your choice.
You better stop harassing me
Or I'll have to switch to voice.

113

Pop Stars

What if pop stars were in band?
What instruments would they play?
How would they be looked at?
Would they be as cool today?

What if life was different?
Like the other way around.
What if band nerds that we've grown to love
Became the stars in town?

Tossing

I spent last week, ALL last week,
Learning to toss my flag.
I threw it up
And now I'm stuck.
My catching's really bad.

Star Quarterback

I'm just a simple quarterback
Who likes to play in the band.
I don't understand why that makes me
Any less of a man.

Score Order

Who made up this order?
I don't understand.
All the small instruments on top,
Of a very big band.

Why are they more important
Then the rest of us here
That they're first on the list,
And the first to appear.

It's not fair I say,
No not fair at all.
This score order thing
Is really just wrong.

They've gone to a new level.
They're really quite unkind.
They say because of the score order,
That they're first in line.

They're first to get a drink,
On the bus, in the door.
They won't give me the time of day,
To say hi is a chore.

It's not fair I say,
No not fair one bit.
That I have to regret
The instrument I picked.

Tuba Dinner

Thanks for coming over here
I'm starving to say the least.
You'll want to get some extra help,
Us tubas like to feast.

For starters I'll take a metric ton
Of chips and spicy sauce.
No I'm not kidding I said a ton
Don't make me get your boss.

For the next three courses bring some rolls
7 white, 5 Rye, 2 Kaiser.
Also bring a truck of chili.
Now for the appetizers.

I'll have a steak, the biggest you got
No actually bring me two.
For sides I'll have a cheeseburger rare
And four pounds of ribs will do.

This all sounds good but not enough
Do you have something filling?
Like a hippo or a humpback whale,
Something definitely worth grilling.

For dessert I'll take it easy.
Like some chocolate flavored moose.
Not the kind in a glass, the kind that eats grass.
Geez you have no use.

There's nothing I enjoy much more
Than a snack to end my day.
Please wrap up all the extra grease
Or I'll refuse to pay.

Soli Solo

Soli Solo I'm next in line.
Soli Solo it is a crime.
Soli Solo we play our scales.
Soli Solo I just might fail.

The Boners

Let me introduce you
To a group of my friends.
They make up their names
And like to pretend
That they're some sort of hero
You think they've outgrown
This childish obsession
About their trombones.

There's Zeus and Juice
And Big Daddy Fly.
Who always just brags
'Bout the size of his "slide."

It never impressed
Lady Laura one bit,
But she did tend to smile
At Booger and Zit.
Of course Dookie and Bird
Just laughed all the time.
And Tinny Fitzgerald,
Well he's into crime.

It's an unusal gang
Of an abnormal brand.
But with no Boners around
The band would be bland.

Sabor Latino

My favorite type of musical style
Is Latin because it moves us.
El Ritmo gets me go'n
Sacudo mis caderas.

Me gusta tocar la trompeta,
And the spanish guitar is sweet.
The style moves mi corazón.
It's a flavor that can't be beat.

O.C.D.

I gotta oil my valves
I gotta gett'm slick.
I have to do it everyday
Or else they're gonna stick.

I scrub them up and down.
I polish day and night.
My instrument is super clean
I finally got it right.

Last Show Of The Year

It's way too cold out here.
Way too cold by far.
My breath I see a mile away.
My snot is forming bars.

My ears are burning, my knees are locked,
It's difficult to swing.
It's hard to do a jazz show,
When these gloves don't mean a thing :)

124

I have to do my solo,
But I'm feeling kinda dumb.
I'm not quite sure what note I'm on,
My lips are totally numb!

Feeling It

Oboes move around too much
When they play with pure emotion.
They say it's 'cause they're "feeling it"
But to me it's just commotion.

       ...oh and sometimes clarinets.

Family

I know we moan and gripe about
How we treat each other.
But the truth is that I really care,
I love you like my brothers.

And whenever things at home get rough
The band room's where I'll be,
To share my life with all of you,
My one true family.

Band Nerds

We're doctors and lawyers
Who did well in school.
We're entrepeneurs
Who own their own pools.

We're accountants, and surgeons
And chem engineers.
We're pitchers and catchers
Who've conquered their fears.

We're colonels and pilots
And designers of trucks.
We're software programmers
With two million bucks.

Music's among us,
Wherever you look,
There's band nerds around us
Even reading this book.

Peace with a whole lotta hair grease.

See ya.

INDEX

A Very Sincere Band Nerd Thank You To:

Mom
Scott
Jessica
Brian Logan
Mike Hurley
Diane Rawlinson
Jason Wick
Louis Kholodovsky
Donald DeRoche
Camilla Stasa
Fran Kick
Scott McCormick
Amy McCabe
Mike Madonia
Dave Morrison
Dan Dougherty
Mike Pickard
Greg Bimm
Meredith Gaffke

To everyone who's shown up for me...I Love You.

CPSIA information can be obtained at www.ICGtesting.com
Printed in the USA
BVOW010558141211

278332BV00004B/7/P